CULTURE MAKES YOU...YOU!

by Carrie Swiger

Illustrations by Maggie Swiger

WestBow Press books may be ordered through booksellers or by contacting:

WestBow Press
A Division of Thomas Nelson & Zondervan
1663 Liberty Drive
Bloomington, IN 47403
www.westbowpress.com
844-714-3454

Interior Image Credit: Maggie Swiger

ISBN: 978-1-6642-9152-2 (sc)
ISBN: 978-1-6642-9154-6 (hc)
ISBN: 978-1-6642-9153-9 (e)

Library of Congress Control Number: 2023902167

Print information available on the last page.

WestBow Press rev. date: 03/10/2023

WESTBOW
PRESS®
A DIVISION OF THOMAS NELSON
& ZONDERVAN

"A friend loves at all times…"
Proverbs 17: 17
(Christian Standard Bible, 2018)

Friendship has many colors,
not only just a few
You can have friends from different
cultures near or far from you

God makes us all special
as only HE can do.

5

Culture is where you come from,
your home, and what you do

Culture is the place you live, the food you eat, and the clothes you wear too

Culture is your family traditions,
those both old and new

God makes us all special as only HE can do.

Your friends can have a
different language, talents,
or what they like to do

Friends come in all shapes
and sizes, with different hair,
skin, and personalities, too

God makes us all special
as only HE can do

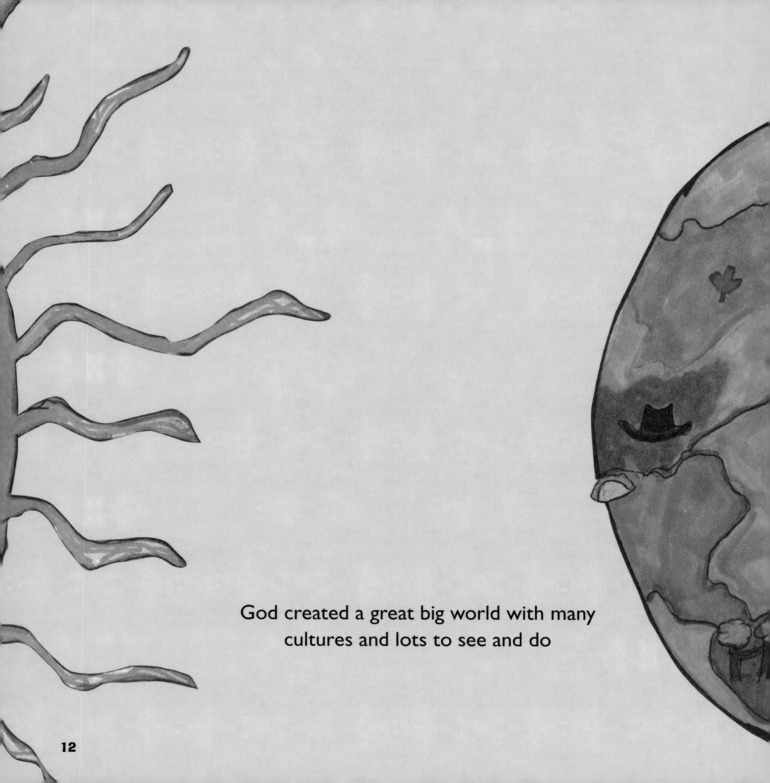

God created a great big world with many cultures and lots to see and do

You can meet friends from a familiar place or explore a culture that is brand new

You can have a friend from a faraway place or one who lives next door to you

God makes us all special as only HE can do.

You can meet a friend anywhere—at school, church, a park, or even at the zoo

Make a friend by introducing yourself and saying, "Nice to meet you"!

God makes us all special as only HE can do.

Friends spend time together playing, laughing, and listening too.

You can share your favorite games and secrets, and they can share theirs with you

Friends are there for each other when you are happy or at times when you are blue

Being there for each other makes
friendship special and true

God makes us all special as only HE can do.

Friendship is like baking, you need the right ingredients— not too many or too few

A cup of love, a heap of understanding, and a spoonful of kindness too

God makes us all special as only HE can do.

There are many ways to show a friend what they mean to you

Trinity ✝ Ranch

Loving friends like God loves us is one thing you can do

24

God created different cultures and friends to
help us, love, learn, and grow, too

Culture is who you are and all the things that make you—YOU!

God makes us all special as only HE can do.

Friendship Prayer

Dear God,

Thank you for the world you made
that is full of cultures near and far
Thank you for the friends I have and the
differences that make them who they are
Thank you for making me unique and giving
me friends that are special and true
Thank you for my friends, their cultures,
what they show me, and all they do
Thank you, God, for teaching me to love
my friends the way that you love me
Thank you for helping me be
the best friend I can be

A-men

About the Author

Carrie Swiger, a professor, writer, and hospitality professional has been helping students and future leaders build their skills relating to service, cultural awareness, community engagement, and performance for many years. She has devoted her career to hospitality and education and has spent over sixteen years in the field of higher education. As a writer, she enjoys writing on topics of cultural awareness and leadership, hospitality and service, community building, and Christian faith. Through her work she has brought a service-minded approach to leadership, creating curricula, strategies, and community-focused initiatives to foster distance learning and genuine understanding.

Carrie grew up in the state of West Virginia and from a young age she realized the importance of hospitality, service, and God's love. Carrie received her BS in Global & Cultural Studies and MA in Global Leadership with a specialization in Higher Education from Crown College and currently works within the community college sector. She believes that there is a substantive connection between education, collaboration, genuine understanding, and the ability to effectively respond to the needs of others. Carrie remains passionate about hospitality, service, leadership, and facilitating responsive environments that are rooted in both collaboration and inclusivity. Additionally, she values the importance of teaching the fundamentals of culture to all ages so that individuals can better understand who they are and also gain an appreciation and love for others. Carrie and her family reside in West Virginia.

Any inquiries can be directed to
E-mail: Carrie.Highercalling@gmail.com